MOGGLEBOX

CHARLIE ELLIS

WHAT CATS REALLY THINK ABOUT TELEVISION

summersdale

MOGGLEBOX

Summersdale Publishers Ltd
46 West Street
Chichester
West Sussex
PO19 1RP
UK

www.summersdale.com

Printed and bound in the Czech Republic

ISBN: 978-1-84953-993-7

Substantial discounts on bulk quantities of Summersdale books are available to corporations, professional associations and other organisations. For details contact Nicky Douglas by telephone: +44 (0) 1243 756902, fax: +44 (0) 1243 786300 or email: nicky@summersdale.com.

You probably think that your cat pays no attention to the programmes you watch; you may even kid yourself that Tiddles and Snowball spend time in the living room because they want to be with you. However, you couldn't be more wrong: cats are telly addicts and there's no denying it. Our team of dedicated researchers have been studying the nation's felines, and we can finally reveal what goes through their moggy minds when they're glued to the tube.

Prepare to be enlightened! And don't even THINK about changing the channel until your four-legged friend has finished watching...

AVOID! AVOID TO ALL OF THEM! I REPEAT: DON'T SNOG, DON'T MARRY, JUST PLAIN AVOID.

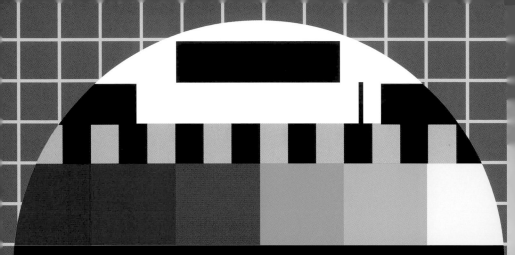

COME ON, LADS!
YOU CAN CLAW ONE BACK!

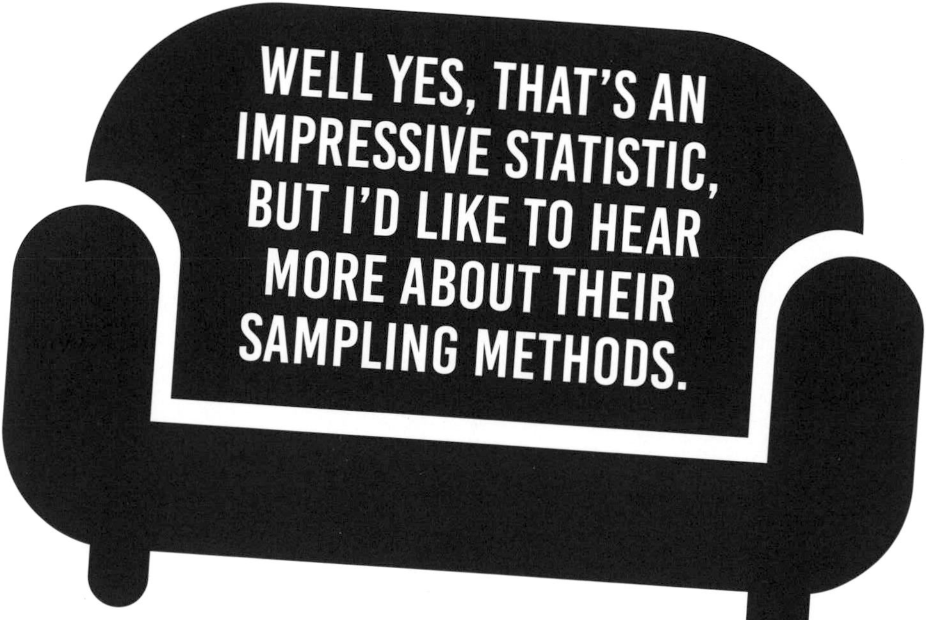
WELL YES, THAT'S AN IMPRESSIVE STATISTIC, BUT I'D LIKE TO HEAR MORE ABOUT THEIR SAMPLING METHODS.

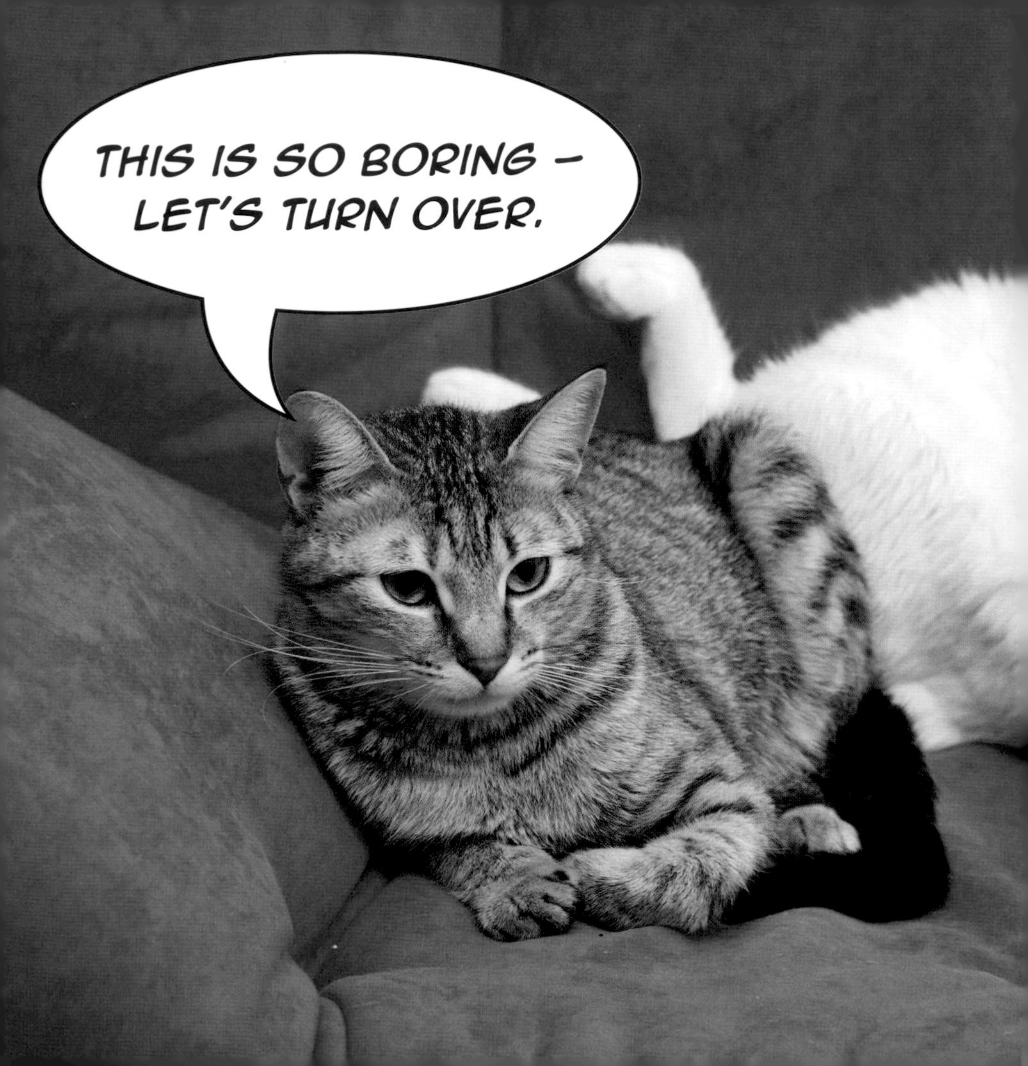
THIS IS SO BORING – LET'S TURN OVER.

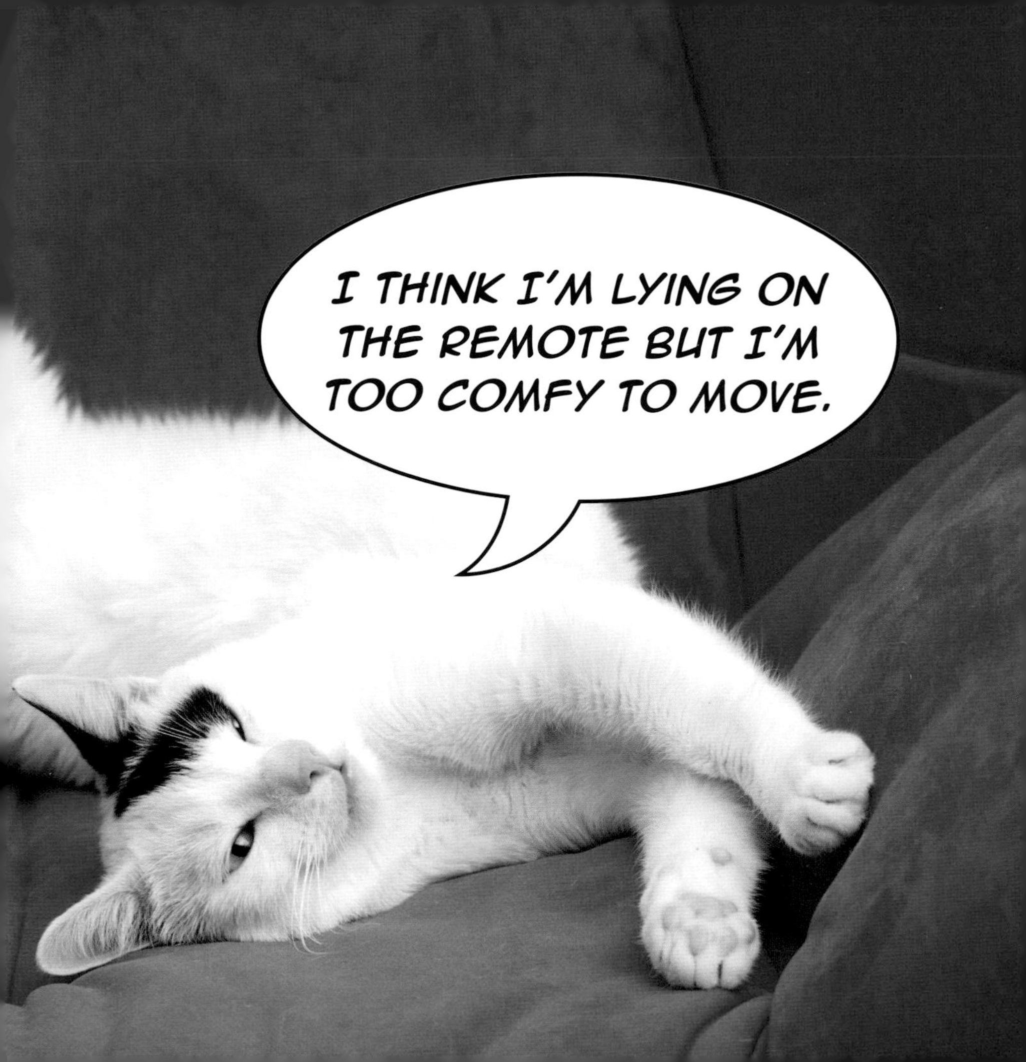
I THINK I'M LYING ON THE REMOTE BUT I'M TOO COMFY TO MOVE.

HURRY UP, KEVIN – *GAME OF THRONES* IS ABOUT TO START!

WATCH EMBARRASSING BODIES, THEY SAID. IT'LL BE FUN, THEY SAID.

IF I JUST STRETCH A *LITTLE* MORE, I CAN REACH THE REMOTE WITHOUT MOVING!

LET ME SEE: ADD THE 10 AND THE 4, MULTIPLY BY 50, AND... OH, THIS IS HARD!

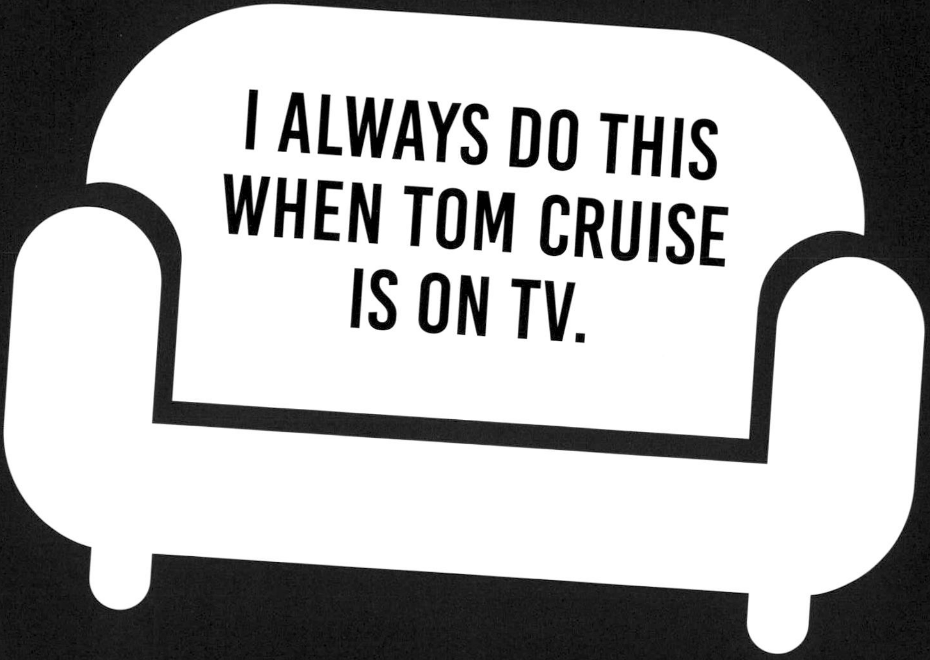
I ALWAYS DO THIS
WHEN TOM CRUISE
IS ON TV.

SOMETIMES A GOOD DOCUMENTARY CAN REALLY MAKE YOU THINK...

IT'S GONNA BE THIS WEEK,
IT'S GONNA BE ME THIS WEEK,
COME ON, LUCKY NUMBERS...

WHY DO I WATCH THIS
EVERY YEAR?
NUL POINTS, CYPRUS.

IT'S NOT CHEATING, MABEL. I JUST LIKE TO BE ABLE TO CHECK MY ANSWERS DURING COUNTDOWN.

IF I HAVE TO WATCH ONE MORE DANCING DOG GETTING THROUGH TO THE FINALS...

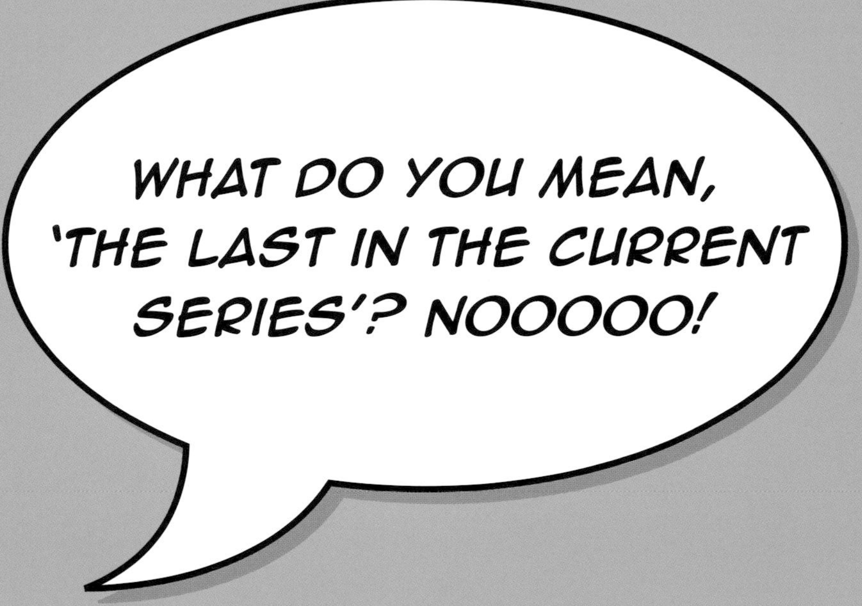
WHAT DO YOU MEAN,
'THE LAST IN THE CURRENT
SERIES'? NOOOOO!

YES, I'M ON A DIET, BUT I CAN WATCH *RICK STEIN'S TASTE OF THE SEA* ALL DAY IF I WANT TO.

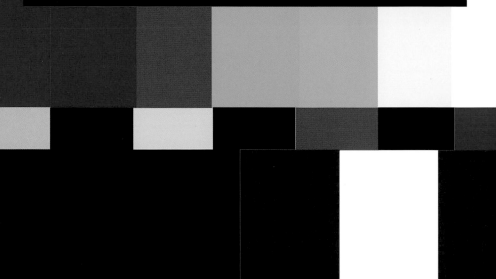

THIS BUSHTUCKER TRIAL IS JUST TOO MUCH.

LOOK, I NEED THE WHOLE SOFA OR I CAN'T STRETCH OUT PROPERLY. YOU'VE GOT A PERFECTLY NICE BLANKET ON THE FLOOR, HAVEN'T YOU?

YES, I DO LIKE TO
KEEP UP WITH THE
KARDASHIANS.
WHAT OF IT?

WELL, I COULD GO OUTSIDE... OR I COULD WATCH ANOTHER EPISODE OF HOMELAND.

WE'RE THINKING OF APPLYING FOR *COUPLES COME DINE WITH ME*, BUT BRIAN NEEDS SOME PERSUADING. DON'T YOU, BRIAN?

HOW TO LOOK GOOD NAKED?
GOK WAN COULD LEARN A FEW
THINGS FROM *ME*, ACTUALLY.

SORRY, I KNOW WE AGREED IT'S YOUR DATE NIGHT TONIGHT, BUT I JUST LOVE SPRINGWATCH. I'M NOT IN THE WAY, AM I?

WHAT DO YOU MEAN THE KILLING HAS BEEN POSTPONED FOR A WEEK DUE TO THE FOOTBALL?

STUCK BETWEEN THESE CUSHIONS?
OH NO, DEFINITELY NOT. I COULD
LEAVE IF I WANTED TO.

(PLEASE HELP ME.)

NOW, ARE YOU SURE YOU DON'T WANT TO THINK TWICE ABOUT CHANGING THE CHANNEL? IT WOULD BE SUCH A SHAME IF THIS LEATHER SOFA GOT... SCRATCHED...

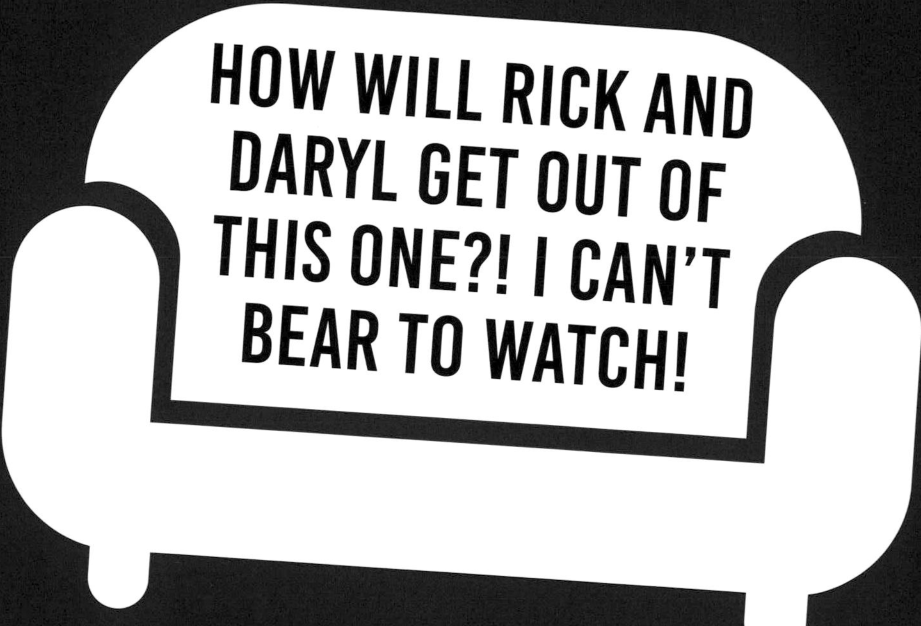
HOW WILL RICK AND DARYL GET OUT OF THIS ONE?! I CAN'T BEAR TO WATCH!

IF ONLY OUR CHAIR SWIVELLED LIKE THOSE ONES, WE WOULDN'T HAVE TO WATCH THIS TRAIN WRECK.

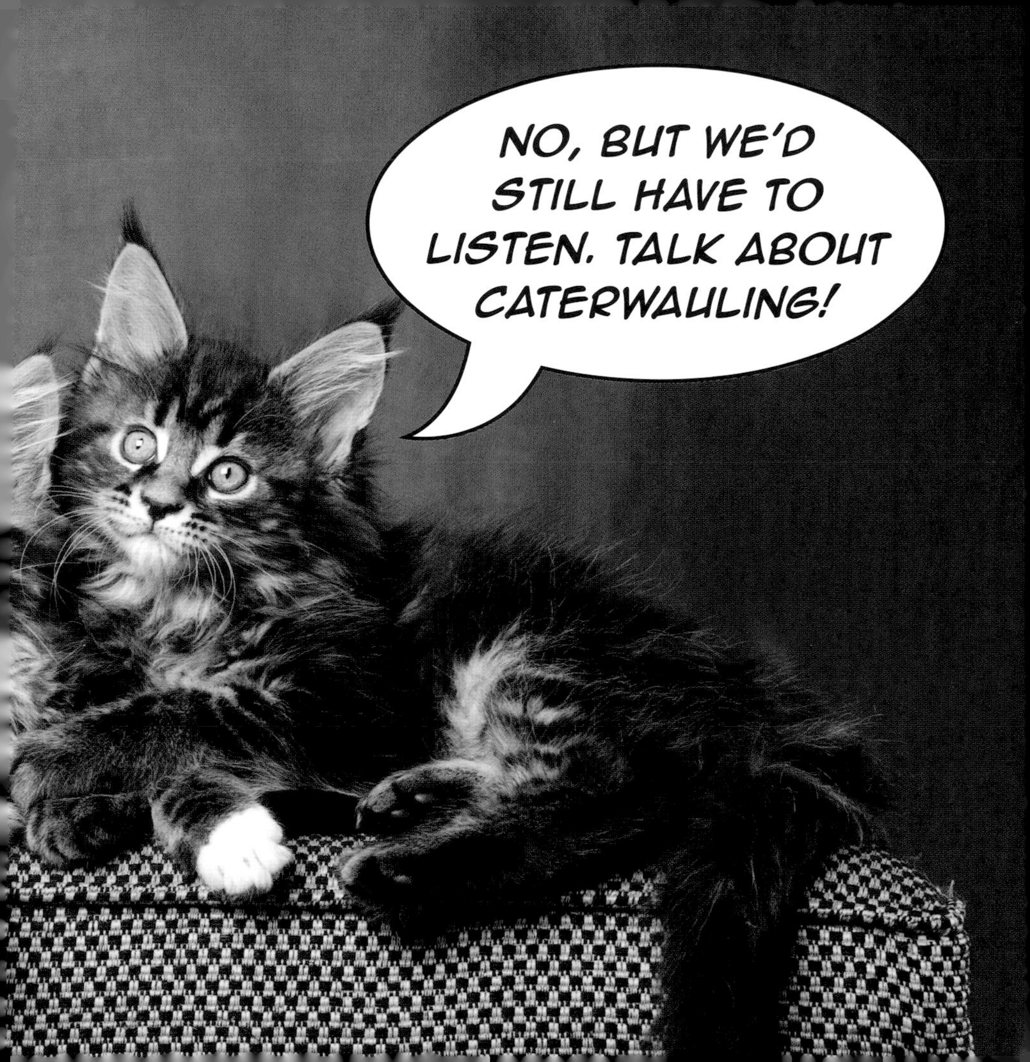
NO, BUT WE'D STILL HAVE TO LISTEN. TALK ABOUT CATERWAULING!

I'M NOT VERY GOOD AT WATCHING HORROR FILMS... CAN YOU HOLD MY PAW?

EXCUSE ME, NOBODY WARNED ME THERE WERE GOING TO BE DOGS IN THIS CRUFTS MALARKEY. TIME TO TURN OVER, I THINK!

I WON'T SLEEP A WINK TONIGHT! I SHOULD NEVER HAVE STAYED UP FOR *TAILS OF THE UNEXPECTED*.

AND, BOOM! HOW'S THIS FOR A POSE? I COULD DO BETTER THAN THOSE GIRLS ON *TOP MODEL* ANY DAY.

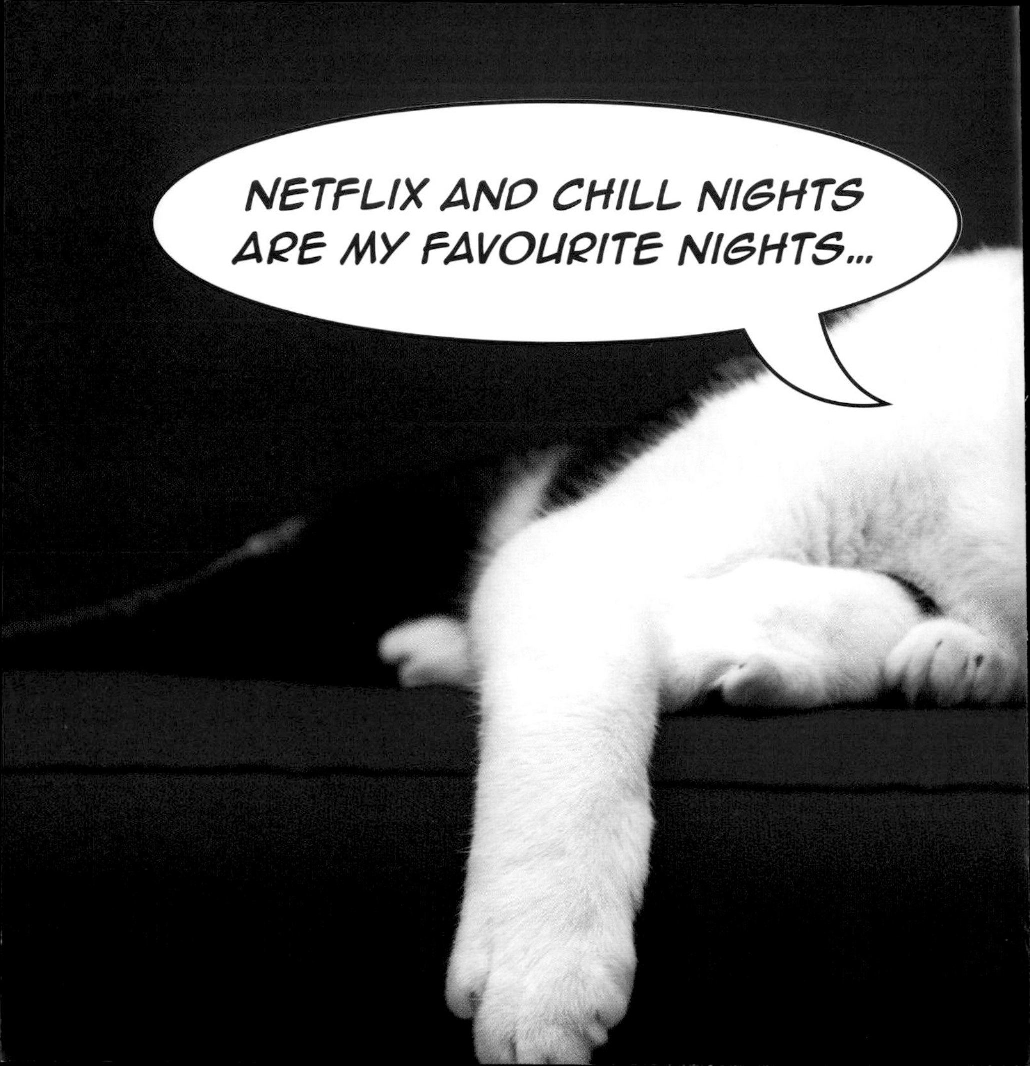
NETFLIX AND CHILL NIGHTS ARE MY FAVOURITE NIGHTS...

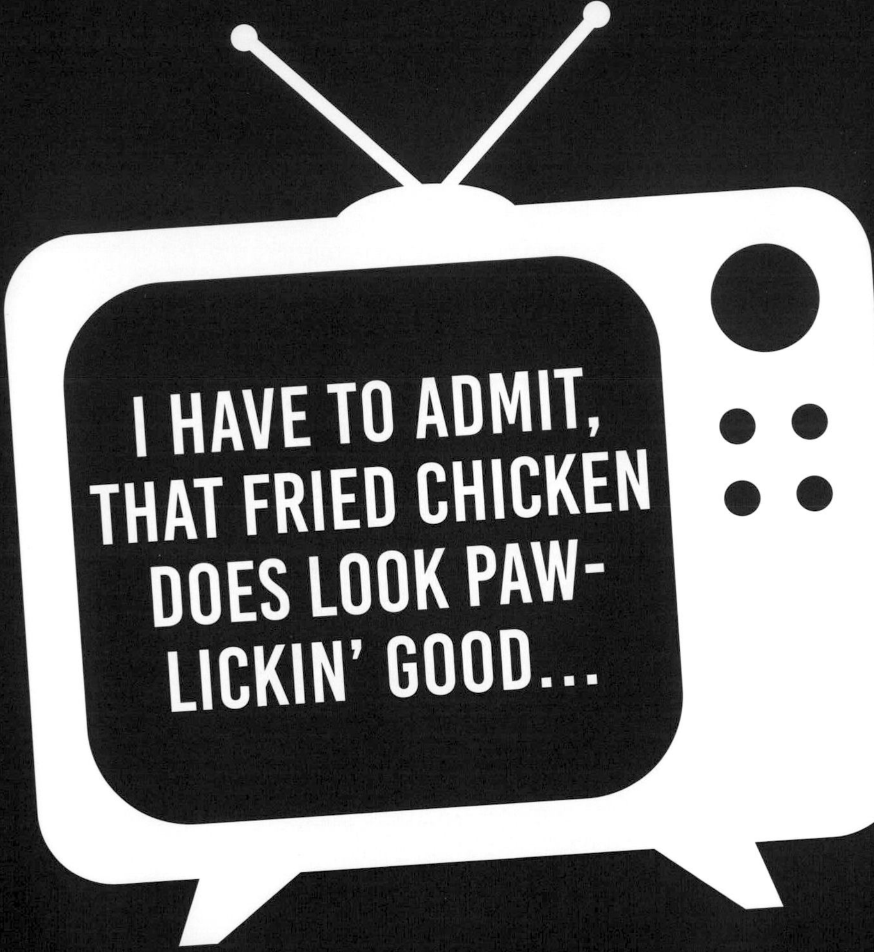
I HAVE TO ADMIT,
THAT FRIED CHICKEN
DOES LOOK PAW-
LICKIN' GOOD...

PLEASE MUM, CAN
I STAY UP TO WATCH THE
RESULTS SHOW JUST
THIS ONCE?

I DON'T KNOW WHY YOU'RE LAUGHING – ISN'T THIS HOW ALL CATS WATCH TV?

COUNTRIES THAT BORDER TURKEY? RIGHT... OOH... I KNOW THIS ONE... I'M SURE I CAN GET A POINTLESS ANSWER THIS TIME!

TWENTY-FOUR-HOUR TV HASN'T AFFECTED US AT ALL, HAS IT, DARLING? DARLING…?

PHOTO CREDITS

If you're interested in finding out more about our books, find us on Facebook at **Summersdale Publishers** and follow us on Twitter at **@Summersdale**.

www.summersdale.com